PHONIC READERS

FOUR SETS OF STORIES FOR CHILDREN

by Barbara Murray

with drawings by Mary Ward Thompson

First published 2002 as four separate booklets by Alpine Books, Greenville, South Carolina, with assistance of Universal Workshop.
2nd printing 2006.
Republished 2013 as a single volume by Universal Workshop.

ISBN 0-934546-64-9

Universal Workshop
Lyme Regis, England, and Raynham, Massachusetts
www.UniversalWorkshop.com
Inquiries: guy@UniversalWorkshop.com

This book is intended to provide interesting and worthwhile stories simply told, using a mostly phonic vocabulary.

The phonic principle

"Phonic" words are those whose spelling keeps to the rules that children have encountered at their stage of learning. The stories will be fun for all children, but they will be especially useful to teachers who use the phonic method for developing children's confidence in reading.

Educators have long debated the merits of the phonic versus the "look-and-say" or whole-word approach. The consensus seems to be that phonic principles best help children toward mastery over the tangle of English spelling. There is now also a realization that those suffering from dyslexia are best helped by phonics.

Color coding

The stories are in four groups, graded for the first four Montessori reading levels. The colors that the Montessori system associates with these levels are red, green, pink, and yellow, so a page with the appropriate color precedes each section.

Note to teachers or parents

A list of "Words to Try" is given before each story or group of stories. These are the few words used in the stories whose spelling goes beyond the phonic rules the children know so far. We suggest that children should have a bit of practice with these words before beginning on the next stories.

Contents

FIRST FABLES

The stories in this section are fables of Aesop.

Words to Try

The Boy and the Nuts

said

half

have

The Ant and the Dove

dove

one

deserves

another

The Wind and the Sun

kindness

works

The Boy and the Nuts

A boy saw a big jar of nuts. He asked his mom, "May I take a handful of nuts?"

"Yes," said his mom.

"As big a handful as I like?" asked the boy.

"As big a handful as you can take," said his mom.

The boy put his hand in the jar. He grabbed a big handful. But when he tried to get his hand out, he found that the neck of the jar was too thin.

He was not able to get his hand out with all the nuts that he held. He tried and tried to squeeze his hand past the neck.

At last he stood there, with his hand still in the jar. He cried and cried. But he still did not wish to let a single nut go.

"You have been tricked by your greed," said his mom. "Pick up a handful that is not as big. Then you can get your hand out of the jar, and you will still have nuts to eat."

Half is better than none.

The Ant and the Dove

An ant needed a drink. He tried to make his way down a blade of grass that grew by a pond. That way he hoped to get to the water. But alas! He slipped and fell into the pond.

On a branch near the pond sat a white dove. She saw the ant fall in, and she felt sad. In a flash, she picked up a leaf with her beak, and let it fall in the pond.

The ant got on top of the leaf raft. Soon he was safe on shore again.

But now the ant saw a man.
The man hid near a tree at the
side of the pond. He threw
down a net to catch the dove.

"O no!" cried the ant. "I will not let you catch the bird that saved my life!"

The ant gave the man a big sting on the leg. "Ouch!" cried the man. He jumped up and down in pain. The bird flew away in the wood.

One good deed deserves another.

The Wind and the Sun

The wind and the sun did not agree. The wind said to the sun, "I am much stronger than you are!"

"Indeed, you are not!" cried the sun.

"Let us have a test, then," said the wind.

"Yes," replied the sun. "Can you see the man down there, on that path? He has on a big, thick coat. Let us each take a turn. We will see if we can make that man take off his coat. If you get him to take his coat off, you win.

If I can, then I am stronger. You may take the first turn."

Then the sun went away under a cloud, and the wind began to blow.

He blew and he blew and he blew.

But the more the wind blew, the more the man hugged his coat round himself. The wind was not able to blow it off.

At last the wind gave up. "You try now," he said to the sun.

The sun came out from under the cloud. He shone and he shone and he shone.

Soon the man on the path got hot. "It is much too hot for this coat!" he said. And he took it off.

Kindness works better than force.

THE QUEEN OF SPAIN
AND OTHER STORIES

"The Queen of Spain" is a legend from the Middle Ages. "Midas" and "Androcles are tales from Greece and Rome.

The Queen of Spain

Words to Say

again   ago   chief

A long time ago the Moors went to Spain. They had a big battle, and took the King of Spain away with them.

The Queen of Spain was sad. She dressed herself like a page boy. She went to the tent of the chief of the Moors and sang to him.

The chief of the Moors liked her song. He made the King of Spain crouch on the ground. He told the Queen she had a King for a footstool. The Queen put her foot softly on the neck of the King.

"I will grant you a wish," said the chief.

"Let me take this King back to his land," begged the Queen.

The wish was granted, and the Queen, still dressed like a boy, led the King to his land.

The first person they met was the Spanish Minister.

"Sire, you must marry again," said the Minister. "The Queen has left you and joined the enemy."

The Minister wanted his own girl to marry the King. But the King did not look at her. He turned to the page boy and said, "Boy, sing me a song."

And the singer sang:

>Down the hills and along the plain,
>Lute in hand, went the Queen of
>   Spain.
>Dressed in the clothes of a boy she
>   went
>And sang in the Moorish chief's own
>   tent.
>He gave her a footstool fair and
>   strong,
>And she got the footstool for a song.

The King then saw that the page boy was his own true Queen. He took her in his arms and they were never parted again.

King Midas and the Wish

Words to Say

ago   golden   **Mi**das   **Pac**tolus
statue   worst

A long time ago there was a king. His name was Midas.

Midas had a big feast for the friend of a god. The god was happy, and he asked Midas to make a wish. Midas did not think very hard. He asked the god to turn all the things he put his hands on into gold.

At first Midas had a lot of fun. He
picked up a leaf. It turned to gold. He
made stones, twigs and flowers turn to
gold too. He sat on his throne. First it
had been wood. Now it was gold.

But alas! Midas soon found out that he was not able to eat. All his food turned into gold. The drink in his cup became solid gold. Midas was hungry and thirsty.

But the worst thing was yet to happen. Midas had a little girl. He loved her very much. When he gave her a hug and a kiss, she turned into a golden statue.

Then Midas saw that he had made a bad and foolish wish. He begged the god to help him.

"I will help you get rid of the wish," the god told him. "Go to the River Pactolus, and wash in the stream."

As soon as Midas washed in the river, all his power to turn things into gold passed to the river. And the river has had golden sands until this day.

Androcles and the Lion

Words to Say

Androcles   arena

Emperor   Roman

Androcles was a poor Roman slave who was taken away to North Africa hundreds of years ago.

His life was hard and painful. His master was cruel. Androcles wished to escape. One dark night he crept out of the house and into open land. He wanted to get to the sea coast. But, by mistake, he found himself in the desert, near a cliff.

He was tired, and crept into a cave to sleep. But soon he was woken by a big roar. A huge lion stood in his way. Androcles was afraid. But the lion held up its paw. In the paw was a big thorn.

Androcles took the thorn out of the lion's paw. The grateful lion limped out of the cave. Soon it came back with a rabbit it had killed. When the poor slave had cooked and fed on the rabbit, the lion led him to a part of the cliffs. A spring of fresh water was gushing from the ground. Androcles was glad to have a drink.

The lion and the man lived with each other for three years. They hunted and slept near each other. But at last Androcles left the cave to find his way back to Rome.

Alas! He was soon captured. In those days slaves who ran away were put in a big arena to be killed by wild beasts.

Androcles was given a lance and pushed into the arena. He shook with terror as a big lion jumped out at him.

But the lion did not spring at him with a roar. It ran up to Androcles and licked him!

It was his old friend! Androcles patted it and leaned on its neck and cried.

The Emperor who ruled Rome was watching the show. He asked Androcles to tell him about the lion. He was so impressed with the tale that he made Androcles a free man.

After that, Androcles used to go round the streets of Rome, and the faithful lion followed him like a dog wherever he went.

THE OLD WOMAN
AND HER PIG

This an old folktale from England.

The Old Woman and Her Pig

Words to Say

all   fright   said   tonight   want
was   water   woman   would

An old woman was sweeping her house, and she found a dime. "I will take this dime to the market," she said, "and get a little pig."

Off she went to the market, and she got a fat little pig. But on the way home the old woman came to a stile, and the little pig would not get over the stile.

Then along came a dog. The old woman said to the dog,

"Dog, dog, bite pig!
Pig will not get over the stile
And I shan't get home tonight."

But the dog would not.

She went on, and she met a stick. She
said to the stick,

"Stick, stick, beat dog!
Dog will not bite pig,
Pig will not get over the stile,
And I shan't get home tonight."

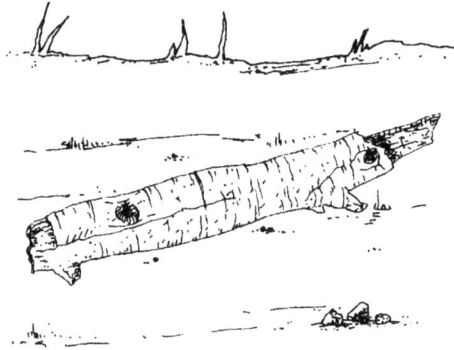

But the stick would not.

She went on, and she met a fire. She
said to the fire,

"Fire, fire, burn stick!
Stick will not beat dog,
Dog will not bite pig,
Pig will not get over the stile,
And I shan't get home tonight."

But the fire would not.

   She went on, and she met a pail of water. She said to the water,

>"Water, water, quench fire!
>Fire will not burn stick,
>Stick will not beat dog,
>Dog will not bite pig,
>Pig will not get over the stile,
>And I shan't get home tonight."

But the water would not.

She went on, and she met an ox. She said to the ox,

"Ox, ox, drink water!
Water will not quench fire,
Fire will not burn stick,
Stick will not beat dog,
Dog will not bite pig,
Pig will not get over the stile,
And I shan't get home tonight."

But the ox would not.

She went on, and she met a man. She said to the man,

"Man, man, slap ox!
Ox will not drink water,
Water will not quench fire,
Fire will not burn stick,
Stick will not beat dog,
Dog will not bite pig,

Pig will not get over the stile,
And I shan't get home tonight."

But the man would not.

   She went on, and she met a rope. She
said to the rope,

"Rope, rope, whip man!
Man will not slap ox,
Ox will not drink water,
Water will not quench fire,
Fire will not burn stick,
Stick will not beat dog,
Dog will not bite pig,
Pig will not get over the stile,
And I shan't get home tonight."

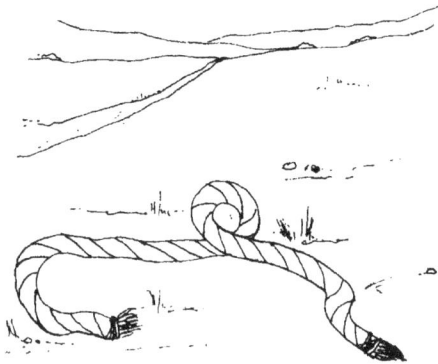

But the rope would not.

She went on, and she met a rat. She said to the rat,

"Rat, rat, chew rope!
Rope will not whip man,
Man will not slap ox,
Ox will not drink water,
Water will not quench fire.
Fire will not burn stick,
Stick will not beat dog,
Dog will not bite pig,
And I shan't get home tonight."

But the rat would not.

She went on, and she met a cat. She said,

"Cat, cat, claw rat!
Rat will not chew rope,
Rope will not whip man,
Man will not slap ox,
Ox will not drink water,
Water will not quench fire,
Fire will not burn stick,
Stick will not beat dog,
Dog will not bite pig,
Pig will not get over the stile,
And I shan't get home tonight."

But the cat said, "If you fetch me a dish of milk, I will claw the rat."

Away went the old woman to the cow.

But the cow said, "Fetch me a wisp of hay, and I will give you the milk."

Then away went the woman to the hay-stack, and she got a wisp of hay for the cow.

As soon as the cow ate the hay, she gave the old woman the milk; and the woman took it in a dish to the cat.

As soon as the cat had lapped up the milk, the cat began to claw the rat.

The rat began to chew the rope.

The rope began to whip the man.

The man began to slap the ox.

The ox began to drink the water.

The water began to quench the fire.

The fire began to burn the stick.

The stick began to beat the dog.

The dog began to bite the pig.

The pig got a fright, and jumped over the stile!

And after all, the old woman did get home that night!

TALES FROM INDIA

The Withered Tree

Words to Say

Be**na**res   India   withered

Near the town of Benares in India, there was a big forest. One noon the god Indra came to walk in it. Indra liked the forest. Even in the gardens of the gods he had not seen leaves more fresh or flowers more fair.

In the midst of the forest he found a huge tree. The tree was withered and rotten. On the tree sat a poor sad parrot.

"Why are you here, foolish bird?" asked the god. "Are there not better trees near by?"

The parrot bowed its head and replied, "O wise god! Under this tree I was born.

From its branches I began to fly. This tree is my friend. Now it is sick and needs me. How can I leave it?"

Indra was filled with pity.

"O bird," he cried, "I wish that men were as true to their friends as you are! Let me grant you a wish."

"Make this tree well again, O wise god!" begged the parrot.

Indra put his hand on the bark of the tree. Then the fungus and mildew dropped away. The rotten leaves fell to the ground. Fresh sap flowed in the branches of the tree, and buds of green and red burst out on every twig.

Now the parrot and the tree were happy again.

The Tiger, the Brahman, and the Jackal

Words to Say

Brahman   tiger   I   so   do
making   said   was   go   me
open   what

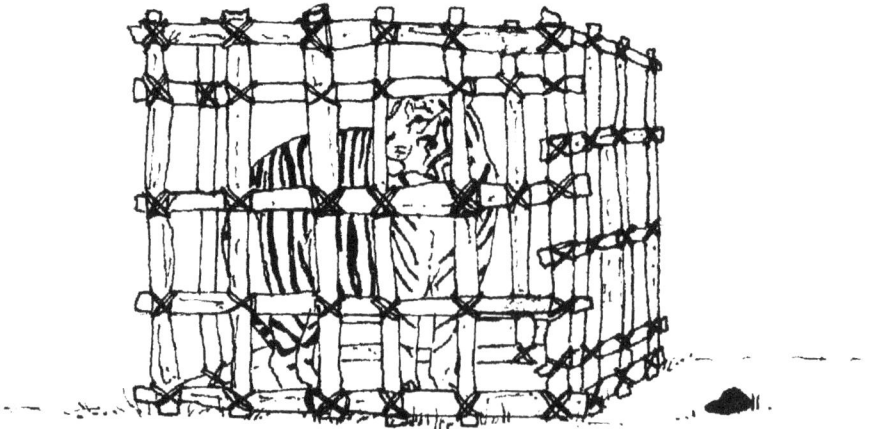

One day a tiger was trapped in a cage. He tried in vain to get out. When he failed, he rolled and bit with rage and grief.

Just then a poor Brahman came along. In India, a Brahman is a wise and good man.

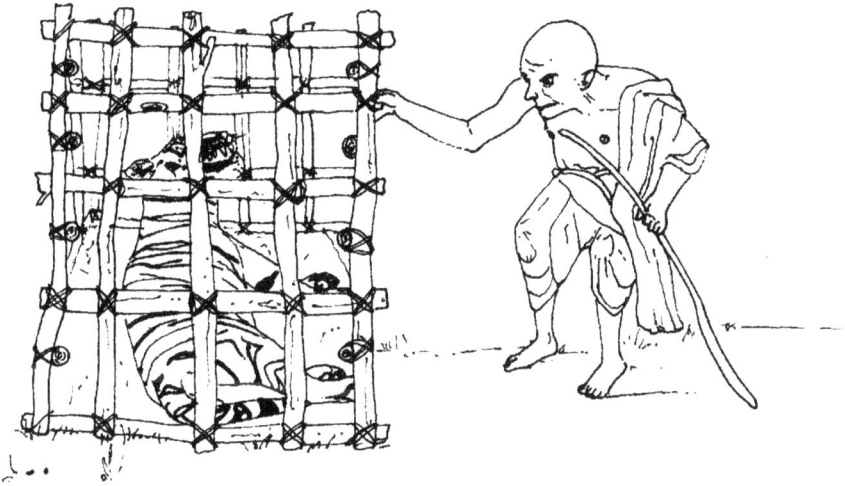

"Let me out of this cage, O wise man!" begged the tiger.

"But if I let you out, you will eat me!" said the Brahman.

"O no!" cried the tiger. "If you let me out, I will be your grateful slave for ever!"

The tiger sobbed and moaned and wept. The Brahman felt quite sorry for him. At last he agreed to open the door of the cage. Out popped the tiger. But the tiger did not thank the Brahman. O no! He grabbed him, and said he would eat him for dinner.

"That is not fair!" cried the Brahman. Now it was his turn to beg the tiger for his life. At last the tiger said, "You may go and ask the first three things you meet if it is fair for me to eat you. If one of them agrees with you, I will spare your life."

The Brahman went off. The first thing he asked was a tree. "I helped the tiger, and now he wants to eat me. Is that fair?" But the tree said, "I give shade and shelter to all who pass. But they tear off my branches to feed cattle. That is not

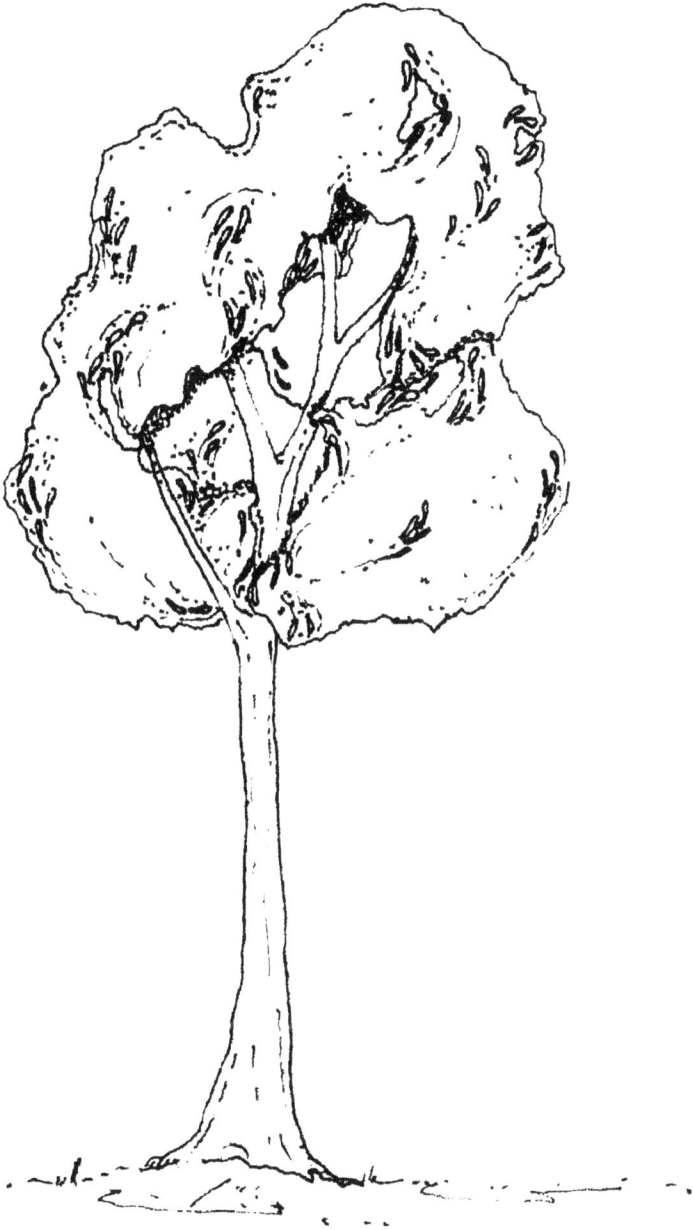

fair. So why do you think the tiger must be fair to you?"

The Brahman was sad at this. He went on till he saw an ox turning a water wheel. But the ox said, "I work hard for very little food. Is that fair? So why do you think the tiger must be fair to you?"

On this the Brahman turned back, very unhappy. But on the way he met a jackal. "What is the matter, sir?" asked the jackal. "You look as sad as a stranded fish!"

The Brahman told him all the story. The jackal looked puzzled. "Tell me again," he said. "I am all mixed up."

By this time the Brahman and the jackal were back at the cage. The tiger was waiting, and making his teeth and claws sharp.

"You have been away a long time!" growled the tiger. "But now let us begin our dinner!"

"*Our* dinner!" said the poor Brahman. "What a strange way to say it!" He felt very scared.

"Give me a little time, my lord, to tell the jackal about this," he begged. "He is a bit slow in his wits."

The tiger agreed, and the Brahman gave the story again, quite slowly.

"O my poor brain!" cried the jackal. "Let me see——how did it begin? You were in the cage, and the tiger came walking by——"

"Nonsense!" said the tiger. "How silly you are! *I* was in the cage!"

"O yes!" cried the jackal, and he acted as if he shook with fright. "Yes——I was in the cage——no, no! Let me see. The tiger was in the Brahman, and the

cage came by——no, that's not it! O
dear! I shall never get it!"

"Yes, you SHALL!" roared the tiger in a
rage. "I'll MAKE you get it! Look here——
I am the tiger——"

"Yes, my lord!"

"And THAT is the Brahman——"

"Yes, my lord!"

"And THAT is the cage——"

"Yes, my lord!"

"And I was in the cage——do you see?"

"But how did you get into the cage?"

"Like THIS!" roared the tiger, jumping into the cage. "NOW do you see?"

"I see very well!" grinned the jackal, as he quickly shut the door. "And now, if you will allow me, I think matters must stay as they were before."

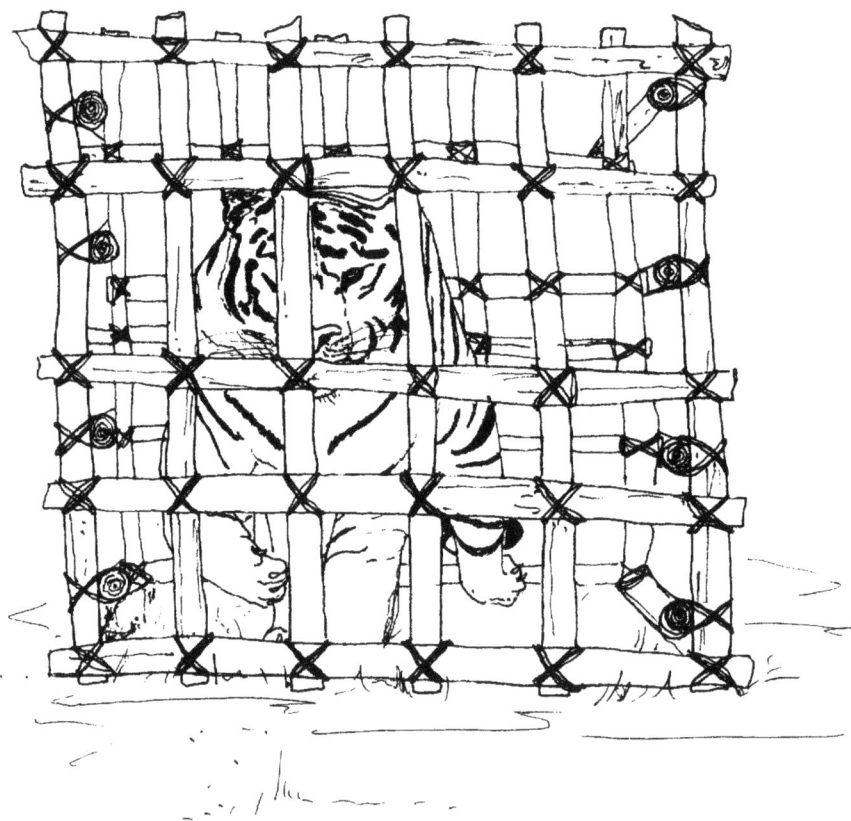